PARENTAL GUIDANCE

How NOT to Raise Your Kids

Remember, your parents didn't have a clue either and you turned out just fine.

THEA MUSSELWHITE

PARENTAL GUIDANCE

Copyright © Thea Musselwhite, 2025

All rights reserved.

No part of this book may be reproduced by any means, nor transmitted, nor translated into a machine language, without the written permission of the publishers.

Thea Musselwhite has asserted their right to be identified as the author of this work in accordance with sections 77 and 78 of the Copyright, Designs and Patents Act 1988.

Condition of Sale
This book is sold subject to the condition that it shall not, by way of trade or otherwise, be lent, resold, hired out or otherwise circulated in any form of binding or cover other than that in which it is published and without a similar condition including this condition being imposed on the subsequent purchaser.

An Hachette UK Company
www.hachette.co.uk

Summersdale Publishers
Part of Octopus Publishing Group Limited
Carmelite House
50 Victoria Embankment
LONDON
EC4Y 0DZ
UK

www.summersdale.com

The authorized representative in the EEA is Hachette Ireland, 8 Castlecourt Centre, Dublin 15, D15 XTP3, Ireland (email: info@hbgi.ie)

Printed and bound in Poland

ISBN: 978-1-83799-565-3
eISBN: 978-1-83799-642-1

This FSC® label means that materials and other controlled sources used for the product have been responsibly sourced

Substantial discounts on bulk quantities of Summersdale books are available to corporations, professional associations and other organizations. For details contact general enquiries: telephone: +44 (0) 1243 771107 or email: enquiries@summersdale.com.

To:

....

From:

....

INTRODUCTION

So, you're a parent. Which means your life mostly comprises sleepless nights, endless piles of dirty laundry, attempts to de-escalate screaming tantrums and watching your house descend into total chaos. But you wouldn't change it for the world, right?! Those little bundles of joy make it all worth it. Well, that, and the wine helps too.

In the following pages you will discover irreverent mothers and fathers whose wisdom is sage, silly and sweary in equal measure. Their wry observations and unique survival tips will help you muddle through each day so that you can become an elite parent, just like them.

Parenthood is wanting to be with your kids forever one minute and wanting to sell them on eBay the next.

Parenting tip:

It's okay to have a break now and then. Send them to the grandparents' house.

Parenting is spending an irrational amount of time trying to convince an already sleepy person to sleep.

Children are like farts...
You can only really
tolerate your own.

If you google your symptoms – tired, messy house, completely broke – it probably just turns out you have kids.

Nowadays, when you get a "booty call", it means it's time to go and wipe someone's bum.

Parenting tip:

Make sure you
child-proof the house.

The most expensive part of having kids is all the wine you have to drink.

You can still do everything you used to do before having kids... it'll just be shit now.

Parenting tip:

When the baby is napping, you should nap. When the baby is eating, you should eat. When the baby is screaming, you should also be screaming.

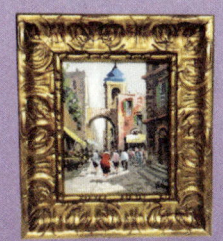

When you're a parent and people ask you what you do for fun...

"I don't know, maybe getting to take a shit on my own."

Parenting tip:

If you're wanting to find a way to get your kids to listen to you, try starting your own YouTube channel.

Now you have your very own

~~poop machine~~

~~puke machine~~

~~sleep thief~~

adorable little baby.

It's okay to have
a favourite child...
whichever one isn't
being a little arsehole.

Parenting tip:

Remind your kids that, because you wiped their arses, they'll have to wipe yours one day too.

Thanks to your kids, now every time you laugh a little bit of pee comes out.

If you can't be a good example, be a terrible warning.

When you're a mum, you have the right to be lazy and braless whenever you find the time.

"Excuse the mess.
My children are
~~making memories~~
being little arseholes."

**Parent sleep:
it's like regular
sleep... but without
the sleep part.**

No matter how cool you used to be, now you're just the snack bitch.

Being a parent is mainly just googling how to do shit.

If other parents smugly tell you their child sleeps all night, you have every right to scream in their face.

Your kids are the reason you live and breathe... and also why you're tired as fuck and your house is a shithole.

You used to
pull all-nighters...
Now you can barely
pull an all-dayer.

No one wants to sleep like a baby (those little buggers never sleep). You want to sleep like a dad.

Parenting tip:

When your kids act like little shits in public, just shout, "Wait until I tell your parents," and pretend they're not yours.

Parenting tip:

Worried they're watching too much TV? Just put the subtitles on and now they're reading!

Shitastrophe:

A poop that escapes the nappy and covers absolutely everything. Every parent will experience this at some point.

Want to raise children *and* have a tidy home? You can't – find a new dream!

**All the best parents
use the F word.**

Remember, your parents didn't have a fucking clue either and you turned out just fine (mostly!).

You've killed every house plant you've ever owned. How the fuck do you keep a baby alive?!

Being a parent
involves waking up
at the arse-crack
of dawn.

There is no greater love than the love a mother has for her wine.

You can say please and thank you a million times and your child will never repeat it. But say "fuck" once...

Although frowned upon, it isn't in fact illegal to call a child an arsehole.

Diamonds used to
be your best friend...
now it's coffee, leggings
and dry shampoo.

Now the kids are in bed you can relax. Just kidding! They're up again!

The only thing more exciting than having a lovely newborn baby is being able to drink again.

Some days they are little angels. Other days you can see why animals in the wild often eat their young.

No one is more full of shit than a parent who just said "maybe".

Are you the perfect parent?

No.

But do you try your best each day to be the perfect parent?

Also no.

If you don't mutter
"for fuck's sake"
under your breath
at least 50 times
a day, are you
even a parent?

They might be little shits, but they're *your* little shits.

Have you enjoyed this book?
If so, find us on Facebook at
Summersdale Publishers, on
Twitter/X at **@Summersdale**
and on Instagram and TikTok at
@summersdalebooks and get in
touch. We'd love to hear from you!

www.summersdale.com